DK READERS

Level 2

Dinosaur Dinners
Bugs! Bugs! Bugs!
Slinky, Scaly Snakes!
Animal Hospital
The Little Ballerina
Munching, Crunching, Sniffing, and
  Snooping
The Secret Life of Trees
Winking, Blinking, Wiggling,
  and Waggling
Astronaut: Living in Space
Twisters!
Holiday! Celebration Days around the
  World
The Story of Pocahontas
Horse Show
Survivors: The Night the
  Titanic Sank
Eruption! The Story of Volcanoes
The Story of Columbus
Journey of a Humpback Whale
Amazing Buildings
Feathers, Flippers, and Feet

Outback Adventure: Australian
  Vacation
Sniffles, Sneezes, Hiccups,
  and Coughs
Starry Sky
Earth Smart: How to Take Care
  of the Environment
Water Everywhere
Telling Time
Ice Skating Stars
Let's Go Riding!
I Want to Be a Gymnast
LEGO: Castle Under Attack
LEGO: Rocket Rescue
Star Wars: Journey Through Space
MLB: A Batboy's Day
MLB: Let's Go to the Ballpark!
¡Insectos! *en español*
¡Bomberos! *en español*
La Historia de Pocahontas
  en español
Meet the X-Men
Spider-Man: Worst Enemies

Level 3

Spacebusters: The Race
  to the Moon
Beastly Tales
Shark Attack!
Titanic
Invaders from Outer Space
Movie Magic
Plants Bite Back!
Time Traveler
Bermuda Triangle
Tiger Tales
Aladdin
Heidi
Zeppelin: The Age of the Airship
Spies
Terror on the Amazon
Disasters at Sea
The Story of Anne Frank
Abraham Lincoln: Lawyer, Leader,
  Legend
George Washington: Soldier, Hero,
  President
Extreme Sports

Spiders' Secrets
The Big Dinosaur Dig
Space Heroes: Amazing Astronauts
The Story of Chocolate
School Days Around the World
LEGO: Mission to the Arctic
NFL: Super Bowl Heroes
NFL: Peyton Manning
NFL: Whiz Kid Quarterbacks
MLB: Home Run Heroes: Big Mac,
  Sammy, and Junior
MLB: Roberto Clemente
MLB: Roberto Clemente
  en español
MLB: World Series Heroes
MLB: Record Breakers
MLB: Down to the Wire: Baseball's
  Great Pennant Races
Star Wars: Star Pilot
The X-Men School
Abraham Lincoln: Abogado, Líder,
  Leyenda *en español*
Al Espacio: La Carrera a la Luna *en
  español*

A Note to Parents

DK READERS is a compelling program for beginning readers, designed in conjunction with leading literacy experts, including Dr. Linda Gambrell, Professor of Education at Clemson University. Dr. Gambrell has served as President of the National Reading Conference and the College Reading Association, and has recently been elected to serve as President of the International Reading Association.

Beautiful illustrations and superb full-color photographs combine with engaging, easy-to-read stories to offer a fresh approach to each subject in the series. Each DK READER is guaranteed to capture a child's interest while developing his or her reading skills, general knowledge, and love of reading.

The five levels of DK READERS are aimed at different reading abilities, enabling you to choose the books that are exactly right for your child:

Pre-level 1: Learning to read
Level 1: Beginning to read
Level 2: Beginning to read alone
Level 3: Reading alone
Level 4: Proficient readers

The "normal" age at which a child begins to read can be anywhere from three to eight years old. Adult participation through the lower levels is very helpful for providing encouragement, discussing storylines, and sounding out unfamiliar words.

No matter which level you select, you can be sure that you are helping your child learn to read, then read to learn!

LONDON, NEW YORK, MUNICH,
MELBOURNE, AND DELHI

Series Editor Deborah Lock
Art Editor Sadie Thomas
U.S. Editor John Searcy
DTP Designer Ben Hung
Production Georgina Hayworth
Picture Researcher Rob Nunn
Illustrator Peter Dennis
Reading Consultant
Linda Gambrell, Ph.D.

First American Edition, 2007
07 08 09 10 11 10 9 8 7 6 5 4 3 2 1
Published in the United States by DK Publishing
375 Hudson Street, New York, New York 10014

Copyright © 2007 Dorling Kindersley Limited

DK books are available at special discounts when purchased in bulk for
sales promotions, premiums, fund-raising, or educational use.
For details, contact:
DK Publishing Special Markets
375 Hudson Street
New York, New York 10014
SpecialSales@dk.com

A catalog record for this book is available
from the Library of Congress

ISBN: 978-0-7566-2948-9 (Paperback)
ISBN: 978-0-7566-2949-6 (Hardcover)

Color reproduction by Colourscan, Singapore
Printed and bound in China by L. Rex Printing Co. Ltd.

The publisher would like to thank the following for their kind
permission to reproduce their photographs.
a=above, b=below, c=center, l=left, r=right, t=top.
Alamy Images: A Room With Views 6-7; Richard Levine 48br.
The Bridgeman Art Library: The Makins Collection 24. **Corbis:**
22br; Bettmann 26; Grace/zefa 4b. Hulton-Deutsch Collection
19tr; Wolfgang Kaehler 14; Markus Moellenberg/zefa 29t; Carl &
Ann Purcell 21bl; Tim Thompson 3cb, 20r; Holger Winkler/zefa
5c. **DK Images:** NASA 28bl, 28cb; National Maritime Museum,
London 2tr, 19tl; Natural History Museum, London 25tr; Stephen
Oliver 15tl, 30cr, 49br; The Science Museum, London 15tr, 18crb.
National Institute of Standards and Technology / NIST: Geoffrey
Wheeler Photography 28tr. **Science & Society Picture Library:**
Science Museum 13cr, 13cra, 13tr. **Science Photo Library:** 16tl.
SuperStock: Maria Ferrari 16-17.

All other images © Dorling Kindersley Limited
For more information see: www.dkimages.com

Discover more at
www.dk.com

Telling Time

Written by Patricia J. Murphy

DK Publishing

Do you know what time it is?
We tell time many times a day.

When is soccer practice?

What time is dinner?

*When does
the party start?*

*What time will
you get there?*

We use clocks to tell time.
They help people plan their day.
People have been telling time
for a long, long time.

Clocks from long ago did not look like ours and they did not keep the best time either.
This is the story of how clocks have changed.

Once upon a time, people woke up when the sun rose and went to bed when the moon and stars came out. These were the first clocks. Sometimes, people used stone pillars to mark the movement of the sun, moon, and stars during the year.

Stonehenge in England

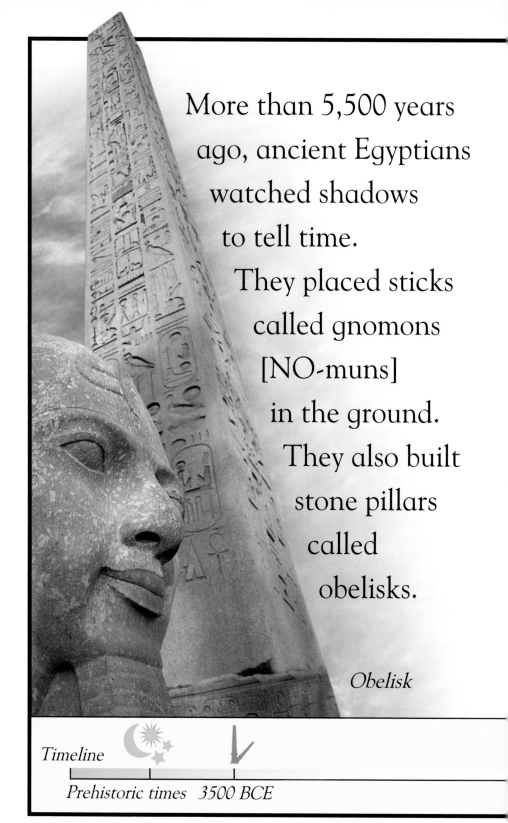

More than 5,500 years
ago, ancient Egyptians
watched shadows
to tell time.
They placed sticks
called gnomons
[NO-muns]
in the ground.
They also built
stone pillars
called
obelisks.

Obelisk

Timeline

Prehistoric times   3500 BCE

These sticks and obelisks cast
long shadows on the ground.
As the sun moved, the direction
of the shadows told people
what part of the day it was.
These devices were
the very first sundials.

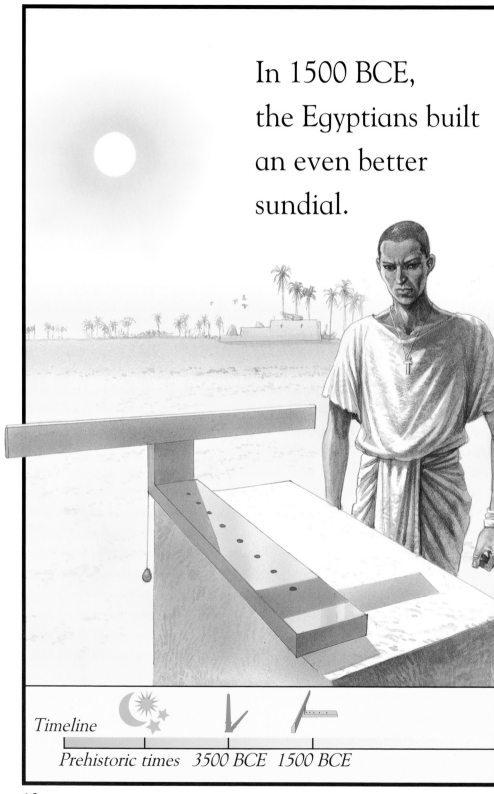

In 1500 BCE,
the Egyptians built
an even better
sundial.

Timeline

Prehistoric times   3500 BCE   1500 BCE

It was shaped like a T and
had special markings.
The marks split the day into
ten hours of daylight and
two hours of twilight.
Like all sundials, this one could
only tell time in sunlight.
People could not tell what time
it was on cloudy days or at night.

Time for bed, Tut!
Around 600 BCE,
Egyptians lined up
merkhets [MER-kets]
with the stars to tell
the time at night.

Starting in 1400 BCE, ancient Egyptians and Greeks used water clocks to tell time during the day and the night.

Timeline

Prehistoric times   3500 BCE   1500 BCE   1400 BCE

Water was poured into a bowl with holes in it. As the water dripped out through the holes, people checked the water levels using special marks. This told them how much time had passed.

Water-level marks

Seven hundred years ago, big and heavy weight-driven clocks were invented. Many of these clocks had round faces and moving hands. After the weights were raised up, they would lower slowly to make the clocks work.

Bells on this clock tower rang on the hour.

Timeline

Prehistoric times   3500 BCE   1500 BCE   1400 BCE   1300

The outside and inside of a pocket watch

Two hundred years later, clocks were made that were powered by springs instead of weights. They were small and light, and some were made to fit in pockets. These tiny timepieces were the first pocket watches.

1500

In 1582, Galileo Galilei noticed that an oil lamp swinging from a chain kept perfect time. He found that a swinging weight always took the same number of beats to go backward and forward.

The cuckoo clock

This pendulum clock makes a whistle that sounds like a cuckoo bird every hour. If it is 12 o'clock, it whistles 12 times!

Another name for a swinging weight is a pendulum.

In 1657, Christiaan Huygens invented a clock that used a pendulum to keep time.

pendulum

1500   1657

On the high seas, sailors needed to know the exact time to find their way.
Pendulum clocks needed to stand still and would not work on choppy waters.

Sands of time

Sometimes, sailors used hourglasses filled with sand or powdered eggshells to tell time. The powder would take one hour to flow from the top bulb to the bottom bulb.

Timeline

Prehistoric times   3500 BCE   1500 BCE   1400 BCE   1300

John Harrison

H4 chronometer

In 1759, John Harrison invented
the H4 chronometer, a special clock
to use on ships.
It worked so well that it won
a prize from the British government.

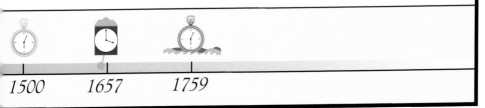

1500   1657   1759

Clocks had problems on land, too. Each town set its clocks using the sun. When the sun reached the highest place in the sky, it was 12 noon for that town.

Since the sun reaches the highest
place in the sky at different times
in different places, every town
had its own 12 noon!
Time was different
all over the place.
It was a mess!

1500   1657   1759

Many people thought it was silly for every town to have its own time. They asked questions like: "How can railroads and mail coaches run on time?" "How can people meet for lunch or do business?" "How can we fix this problem?" Sandford Fleming, a railroad worker, knew the answer.

Greenwich Mean Time
Greenwich Mean Time (GMT) is the time in Greenwich, England. Each time zone was described by how many hours away from GMT it was.

Royal Observatory Greenwich

Timeline

Prehistoric times   3500 BCE   1500 BCE   1400 BCE   1300

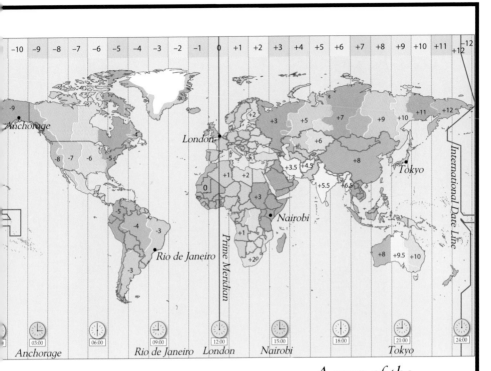

A map of the world's time zones

His idea was to divide the world into 24 time zones. Each zone was exactly one hour apart from its neighbors. Now, time was the same for everyone in each zone.

1500　　1657　　1759　　1884

In the 1880s, women were
the first to wear wristwatches.
After soldiers wore them in
World War I, men liked
to wear them as well.

Timeline

Prehistoric times   3500 BCE   1500 BCE   1400 BCE   1300

Later, watches with tiny quartz crystals inside would become the best timekeepers. The crystals moved like pendulums, but kept even better time. Quartz watches are still popular today.

Quartz crystal

Quartz watch

Digital quartz watches
In 1972, quartz watches went digital. A display of numbers appeared instead of a clock face.

1500   1657   1759   1884   1885

The first
atomic clock

Quartz watches no longer keep
the most exact time.
What does?
Atomic clocks do!
Atomic clocks use atoms—
tiny particles, too small for us
to see—to help tell time.
The atoms act like pendulums.
They move backward and forward
billions of times per second.
This lets atomic clocks tell time
to a billionth of a second.

*Modern atomic
wristwatch*

| 1500 | 1657 | 1759 | 1884 | 1885 | 1949 |

Space travel

So, why do we need to tell time to a billionth of a second?

Satellites

Radio and television broadcasts

Many forms of
technology that
we use today need
the split-second time
of an atomic clock
to work.

These pages show
just a few examples.

*Cell
phones*

Today, clocks come in all shapes, sizes, colors, and styles. Some flash, make sounds, play music, or say the time out loud. Others time how fast you run.

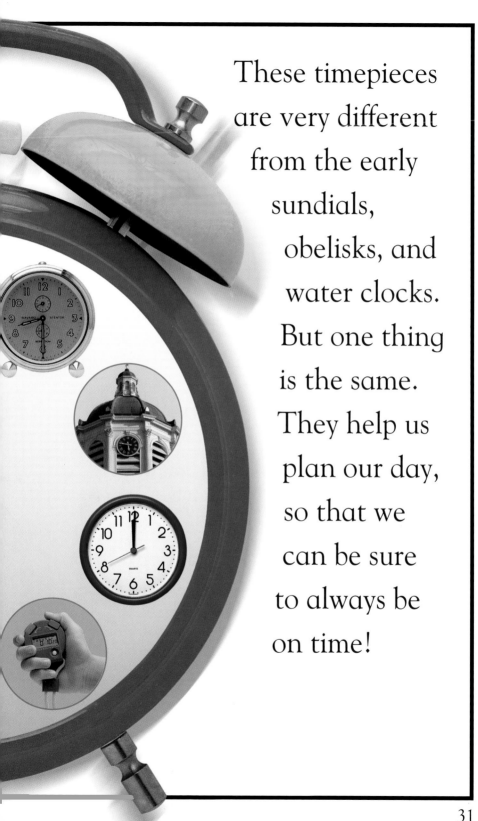

These timepieces are very different from the early sundials, obelisks, and water clocks. But one thing is the same. They help us plan our day, so that we can be sure to always be on time!

Timely facts

Long-case clocks were built to hide their long pendulums. The song "Grandfather's Clock" written in 1876, inspired people to call them grandfather clocks.

The ancient Egyptians were the first people to divide the hour into 60 parts, or minutes. Their number system was based on the number 60, which is easy to divide by 2, 3, 4, 5, and 10.

The world's smallest clock is an atomic clock the size of a grain of rice created by the National Institute for Standards and Technology in Boulder, Colorado, in 2004.

The Colgate Palmolive clock is one of the world's biggest clocks. It measures 55 feet (16.8 m) around! It is located in Jersey City, New Jersey. It was built in 1924.

Colgate

Index

3 Vols. 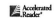 **6023-26**

DK Readers Level 3
Publisher **DK Publishing, Inc.**

Gumdrop Price $44.85

Trade Binding

Title	Dewey	©	Item Price
Fantastic Four: The World's Greatest Superteam	791	2007	$14.95
School Days: Around the World	Juv	2007	$14.95
Story of Chocolate	641	2005	$14.95

USA248AR6.5

6 Vols. **6024-25**

DK Readers Level 4
Publisher **DK Publishing, Inc.**

Gumdrop Price $79.70

Trade Binding
Reviews: BL, HG, SLJ

Title	Dewey	©	Item Price
📕 📗 Dinosaur Detectives	560	2001	$12.95
Flash's Book of Speed	531	2005	$12.95
Green Lantern's Book of Inventions	600	2005	$12.95
📗 Megatron Returns	Fic	2005	$12.95
📕 📗 Micromonsters: Life Under the Microscope	595	1999	$12.95
Thomas Edison: The Great Inventory	Juv	2007	$14.95

USA248AR5.5-5.8RC4.1-4.9

• prepub
Titles may be purchased individually.